POETRY ODYSSEY

Edited By Andrew Porter

First published in Great Britain in 2022 by:

Young Writers
Remus House
Coltsfoot Drive
Peterborough
PE2 9BF
Telephone: 01733 890066
Website: www.youngwriters.co.uk

All Rights Reserved
Book Design by Ashley Janson
© Copyright Contributors 2021
Softback ISBN 978-1-80015-776-7

Printed and bound in the UK by BookPrintingUK
Website: www.bookprintinguk.com
YB0493J

FOREWORD

For Young Writers' latest competition This Is Me, we asked primary school pupils to look inside themselves, to think about what makes them unique, and then write a poem about it! They rose to the challenge magnificently and the result is this fantastic collection of poems in a variety of poetic styles.

Here at Young Writers our aim is to encourage creativity in children and to inspire a love of the written word, so it's great to get such an amazing response, with some absolutely fantastic poems. It's important for children to focus on and celebrate themselves and this competition allowed them to write freely and honestly, celebrating what makes them great, expressing their hopes and fears, or simply writing about their favourite things. This Is Me gave them the power of words. The result is a collection of inspirational and moving poems that also showcase their creativity and writing ability.

I'd like to congratulate all the young poets in this anthology, I hope this inspires them to continue with their creative writing.

CONTENTS

Co-Op Academy Nightingale, Harehills

Amir Ismail (10)	1
Adam Fiaz (10)	2
Michael Owusu Nsiah Opoku (10)	3
Jessica Nolan (10)	4
Alaa Ismail (9)	5
Gabriella Nti Gyimah (9)	6
Alannah Grant (9)	7
Sunny Sharma Vashishat (9)	8
Daniella Nti Gyimah (8)	9
China-Rose Lewis O'Leary (9)	10

Hob Moor Community Primary School, Acomb

Zara Brolly (8)	11
Niamh Parrott (7)	12
Lincoln Sketcher (7)	13
Harper Knaggs (9)	14
Laila Hewitt (8)	15
Sofia Lund (7)	16
Matty Allen (7)	17
Oscar Deighton (7)	18
Alan Kwiecien (9)	19
Lottie Legg (8)	20
Ella-Mai Watson (8)	21
Amelia Brooks (8)	22
Dylan Greer (8)	23
Jacob Speck (7)	24
Nicky Howes (8)	25

Rawdhatul Uloom Primary School, Burnley

Laiba Abbas (10)	26
Imaan Fatima (10)	27
Mariah Mirza (7)	28
Adil Ahmed (10)	29
Maryam Mirza (9)	30
Basil Yousaf (9)	31
Abdul Rahmaan Arslan (9)	32
Ibrahim Shakeel (7)	33
Zubaidah Parveen (9)	34
Nusaybah Raees (9)	35
Halimah Mahmood (10)	36
Safa Afzal (7)	37
Amirah Hussain (9)	38
Muhammad Umar (7)	39
Laiba Bi (10)	40
Talha Ali (7)	41
Sana Mirza (9)	42
Aysha Dean (9)	43
Zulekha Parveen (10)	44
Maryam Noor (9)	45
Faatimah Arslan (7)	46
Rayhaan Shaikh (7)	47
Abudrda Mirza (9)	48

St Margaret's Primary Academy, Lowestoft

Lilly Deeks (10)	49
Lola-Rose Heslop (9)	50
Louis Freeman (10)	51
Cara Blevins (8)	52
Erin Golds (9)	53
Jared Brooks Savage (8)	54

Dylan Wood (9)	55	Ryan Arlow (9)	99
Alfie Hopkins (10)	56	Daniella Pasquale (9)	100
Thomas Shackleton (9)	57	Connor Hopkins (9)	101
Cohen Kirk (8)	58	Clara Westgate (10)	102
Tommy Buckle (8)	59	Ellah-Maye Serina Johnston (9)	103
Zoe Morris (8)	60	Oscar Cushion (9)	104
Lois	62	Alivia Dixon	105
Finley Wilton (10)	63	Lennie Hodges (7)	106
Logan Winyard (9)	64	Eeridesu Cetin (8)	107
Joseph Knight (9)	65	Levi Stanborough (10)	108
Jemima Pomfrett (8)	66	Frankie Yeo (8)	109
Finlay-Jack Page (9)	67	Scarlett Lee-Hagger (9)	110
Daisy McLelland (9)	68	Isabelle Girling (8)	111
Junior Hayden-Hindes (10)	69	Teesha Liburd (7)	112
Mila Lubbock (9)	70	Faith Pearce (8)	113
Kayla Louise (9)	71	Charlie Reeves	114
Kaitie-Jade Stockley (7)	72	Alice Burbridge (10)	115
Henley Brown (9)	73	Ellie Davies (11)	116
Noah McCondochie (9)	74	Logan Caulkin (9)	117
Alfie McIvor (9)	75	Brooke-Leigh Layton (7)	118
Nell Hickinbotham (10)	76	Jasmin Walpole (10)	119
Imogen Allison (10)	77	Lucy Stammers (10)	120
Maddison Hopkins (9)	78	Roman Morris (9)	121
Daisy-Rae Taylor (9)	79	Shane Gibbs (10)	122
Maisy Clements (8)	80	Kasey-Ann Nwaefuna (8)	123
Kyle Charlton (9)	81	Ethan Hemsley (11)	124
Poppie Nash (8)	82	Thomas Copeman (9)	125
Mary-Jane Grammage (10)	83	Lola Nash (8)	126
Fynley Dowler (10)	84	Myles Lloyd (7)	127
Hallum Magee (10)	85	Riley Hayden Hindes (8)	128
Mollie Shaw (8)	86	Daniel Gadney (11)	129
Tiffany Rogers (7)	87	Kieren Bollans (10)	130
Eavan White (9)	88	Lottie Beresford (9)	131
Parker Jeffs (7)	89	Amelia-Lloyd Lloyd (8)	132
Aden Moyse (10)	90	Jacob Bale (10)	133
Isabella Smith (7)	91	Dalton Welton (10)	134
Tilley Beresford (11)	92	Tilly (10)	135
Lacey McIvor (7)	93	Owen Smith (8)	136
Tyler Hutcheson (9)	94	Mason Clemens (10)	137
Taylor Louch (9)	95	Scarlett Griffin (9)	138
Holly Dyer (8)	96	Hayden Kirk (10)	139
Eve-Louise Chapman (11)	97	Rhian Majoram (10)	140
Scott Ardley (10)	98	Leah Grimmette (10)	141

Mia Wright (10)	142
Stephan Ferreira	143
Gracie Bloomfield (9)	144
Aslan Cetin (10)	145
Malaja White (10)	146
Roxy Porter (8)	147
Ellie Potter (7)	148
Bailey Blowers (8)	149
Lilly Burbridge (10)	150
Samantha Macpherson (8)	151
Kal Davidson (8)	152
Rihann Forder	153
Paige Louch (6)	154
Grace Copeman (7)	155
Gohul (7)	156
Emily Smith (8)	157
Holly Ellen Ralph (8)	158

Tickton CE Primary School, Tickton

Imogen Cowan (7)	159
Thea Parker (7)	160
Florence Fawke (9)	161
Esmay Martin (8)	162
Eva Fisher (8)	163
Ewan Pottage (7)	164
Abigail Hadfield (8)	165
Molly Harrison (7)	166
Lucy Harling (7)	167
Layla Adams (8)	168
Lily Coates (7)	169
Bobby Butler (7)	170
Henry Fisher (7)	171
Arthur Hornby (7)	172
Tom Jebson (7)	173
Logan Butler (8)	174
Daisy Cowell (7)	175
Phoebe Gibson (7)	176
Mollie Gillyon (8)	177
Miley Wright (7)	178
Frankie Sheppard (7)	179
Ava Melling (7)	180
Myles Musgrave (7)	181

Emmy Harrison Saunders (7)	182
Poppy Smith (7)	183
Anna Gibson (8)	184
Alissia Williams (9)	185
Rosie Smith (9)	186
Riley Coates (8)	187
Henry Leek (7)	188
Phoebe Dawson (7)	189
Chantelle Stewart (8)	190
Ted Plant (9)	191
Ella Hadley (8)	192
Annie Moody (7)	193
Jack Cawkwell-Jeffrey (7)	194
Lyla Thomson (8)	195
Hollie Taggart (8)	196
Sebby Holmes Rodmell (8)	197
Isla Murphy (8)	198
Charlie Hague (8)	199

Ysgol Cae Top, Bangor

Layla Williams (9)	200
Sofia Roque-Nunes (9)	201
Evangeline Goodwin (10)	202
Hazel Story (10)	204
Osian Layton (9)	205
Flora Carré (9)	206
Abirami Nadarajah (9)	207

THE POEMS

The Airport Traveller

I'm on a plane, going to Ukraine
In a hotel, having lunch in a fancy place in Dubai
Enjoying life, going to the gym after
Then going to a fair to eat a pear
Blowing on some bubbles
Going in the blue sky
Glowing in a fair
Going on a roller coaster
Let's get going
On the way to a different country
Flowing with the view and going to the moon
Slowing down after fast movement and having breaks
Back flowing while I swim on a hot, wonderful day
Mind-blowing views that people could see in the distance
Overflowing in the beach with friends and family
All-knowing what we're doing for delicious dinner when snowing in the UK in December
Was fun, let's get going
Oh, the brilliant time that we had.

Amir Ismail (10)
Co-Op Academy Nightingale, Harehills

Howzat?

Here he is, with bat and ball,
Playing cricket on a dusty pitch,
Three wooden stumps and a sturdy base,
Now... *Smash!*
The fielders are all on the chase!

Sauntering along the emerald grass,
A spinmeister prepares, ball in hand,
The withered seam woven as train tracks,
Just then, the ball is released,
The willowed bat makes contact and *crack!*

At midnight, he is still on strike.
Hitting all the balls with style and might,
Then a new bowler steps in,
He bowls a screamer of a ball and...
The finger is raised! It's a win!

Adam Fiaz (10)
Co-Op Academy Nightingale, Harehills

The Wrong And Smooth Treasure

Whose treasure is that? I think I know,
Its owner is quite sad though.
It really is a tale of woe,
I watch him frown, I say hello.
He gives his treasure a shake,
And sobs until tears he makes.
The only other sound's the break
Of distant waves and birds awake.
The treasure is wrong, smooth and deep,
But he has promises to keep.
Until then, he shall not sleep,
He lies in bed with ducts that weep.
He rises from his bitter bed,
With thoughts of sadness in his head.
He idealises being dead,
Facing the day with never-ending dread.

Michael Owusu Nsiah Opoku (10)
Co-Op Academy Nightingale, Harehills

How To Make Jessica

Take
The moves of a fish,
The twists and turns of a worm
And the glides of a shark
For the moves.

Take
The skinniness of a straw,
The paleness of wax melts
And the hairiness of a gorilla
For the body.

Take
The gingerness of a cat,
The blondeness of the sand
And the brownness of mud
For the hair.

Take
The juiciness of an apple,
A nose as cute as a button
And the shine of a star
For the lips, nose and eyes.

Jessica Nolan (10)
Co-Op Academy Nightingale, Harehills

Yearning For Summer

During a cold, nasty winter, I'm yearning for summer.
All this snow, slush and ice, it's really a bummer,
Kick the snowshoes and skis,
Slick boards out the door.
Banish the short, gloomy days; hey, winter's a bore!
Sunny rays warming me, bring on the heat!
Lazy time on a sandy beach, just can't be beaten.
When it all starts to thaw, and spring in a corner,
Oh, hurry up! Hurry up!
Please, give me summer!

Alaa Ismail (9)
Co-Op Academy Nightingale, Harehills

A Joyful, Happy Child

I'm a good and brilliant child,
I live in a purple little home,
With a big tree outside.

When I laugh I make people happy,
When I smile I light up the room,
I am smart and can do many things,
I laugh and play the whole day long,
I hardly cry.

I have a big tree in front of my house to shade me from the sun.
And under it, I often sit when all my play is done.

A happy, joyful child I am!

Gabriella Nti Gyimah (9)
Co-Op Academy Nightingale, Harehills

A Poem About Myself

Hello, I'm going to tell you a bit about myself,
So sit back, relax, and take a snack...

What I like to do is play outside and hide from others to scare them.
My other thing I like to do is build,
After that I like to chill and eat cake.
I like learning other things like maths, English and science
Finally I do what I can to be the best at who I want to be.

Alannah Grant (9)
Co-Op Academy Nightingale, Harehills

A Bird That Sees Three Other Birds

Once there was a bird,
He chirped some words,
He stopped chirping.

He saw a parrot,
It was in the park,
Next to it was a dog, barking like an alarm.

After, he saw a flamingo,
It was standing on a mango,
He was going to see his friend.

Finally, he saw an owl,
It was covered with a towel,
It was tooting in the night.

Sunny Sharma Vashishat (9)
Co-Op Academy Nightingale, Harehills

Thanksgiving

First, we give thanks to God,
For the food that we are given.
Then we give thanks for the house,
The house that we live in.
Then we give thanks for the sun,
That shines above us.
But mostly, we give thanks for the people that we love and who love us back!

Daniella Nti Gyimah (8)
Co-Op Academy Nightingale, Harehills

My Sister

M arvellous but mischievous
I ntelligent like a scientist
L oud as a lion
A s bright as the sunshine.

M oody on Mondays
A s helpful as Mummy
E nergetic like a bouncy ball.

China-Rose Lewis O'Leary (9)
Co-Op Academy Nightingale, Harehills

This Is Me

T alented, Fortnite player, rugby player,
H appy, caring, helpful, kind,
I am as fast as a cheetah on weekends,
S kipping is my favourite thing to do.

I am as slow as a sloth on school days,
S wimming is my favourite thing to do.

M y friends' names are Amelia and Maya, they are amusing,
E ager, I am as strong as a gorilla on weekends.

Zara Brolly (8)
Hob Moor Community Primary School, Acomb

This Is Me

T alented swimmer,
H elpful, happy, kind, caring,
I am a cheetah on my bike or scooter,
S wimming is my hobby, and snacks.

I am a pretty flower,
S hiny when I get out of the shower.

M y name is Niamh and I am nice,
E ager, I am as loud as a firework, I am as kind as animals.

Niamh Parrott (7)
Hob Moor Community Primary School, Acomb

This Is Me

T alented Fortnite player.
H elpful, good, happy, kind, caring.
I am cool as a gorilla.
S mooth as a bear.

I am as fast as a cheetah.
S coffed my snacks, I am as smart as a white gorilla.

M y name is Lincoln, I am lucky and loyal.
E nthusiastic, I am as smart as a chameleon.

Lincoln Sketcher (7)
Hob Moor Community Primary School, Acomb

This Is Me

T alented at rugby
H arper is my name, helpful and happy
I am bright like a cherry
S mart, sweet.

I am a bouncy ball skipping
S chool is the best, swimming is good for you.

M y name is Harper, happy, helpful
E ager, I am as fast as a cheetah.

Harper Knaggs (9)
Hob Moor Community Primary School, Acomb

This Is Me

T alented roller skater,
H elpful, happy and kind,
I 'm a freezing winter morning,
S mart, that's me.

I 'm a big, great sunflower,
S coffing my snacks.

M y name is Laila, loud and loving,
E ager as a child trying to get their toys.

Laila Hewitt (8)
Hob Moor Community Primary School, Acomb

This Is Me

T alented dancer,
H ave fun like a dog,
I am a cheeky girl,
S o silly spectating sport.

I am a pretty flower on a sunny day,
S wimming in the scorching summer sun.

M y favourite food is chicken nuggets,
E xcellent at exercise.

Sofia Lund (7)
Hob Moor Community Primary School, Acomb

This Is Me

T alented rugby player
H appy, grateful, helpful
I am as fast as a cheetah
S kipping all the way to school.

I am a ray of sunshine
S weet as sugar.

M atty is my name, marvellous and mindful
E ager, I am as sneaky as a snake.

Matty Allen (7)
Hob Moor Community Primary School, Acomb

This Is Me

T alented, Fortnite player.
H appy, helpful and kind.
I am a cheetah.
S wimming is what I love.

I am as tricky as lightning.
S mart.

M y name is Oscar, orangutan.
E ager, I am as fast as a Formula One.

Oscar Deighton (7)
Hob Moor Community Primary School, Acomb

This Is Me

T alented rugby player
H appy, kind horse rider
I am a cheetah
S mart, that is me.

I am a lightning bolt
S mooth like Hershey's.

M y name is Alan, ambitious
E ager, I am as sneaky as a chameleon.

Alan Kwiecien (9)
Hob Moor Community Primary School, Acomb

This Is Me

T alented horse riding
H appy, kind, helpful
I am as soft as a sofa
S nacks are yummy.

I am a ray of sunshine
S wimming, I love.

M y name is Lottie, I love lakes
E ager, I am as quiet as a mouse.

Lottie Legg (8)
Hob Moor Community Primary School, Acomb

This Is Me

T alented penny boarder
H appy, helpful, caring
I am a happy girl
S mart and sweet.

I am beautiful
S chool is really fun.

M y name is Ella-Mai
E ager, I'm as happy as a flower.

Ella-Mai Watson (8)
Hob Moor Community Primary School, Acomb

This Is Me

T alented singer
H appy, helpful
I am as sweet as a cherry
S chool is cool.

I am pink
S kateboarding is my hobby.

M y name is Amelia, amazing
E ager I am, as wise as an owl.

Amelia Brooks (8)
Hob Moor Community Primary School, Acomb

This Is Me

T alented writer.
H elpful as can be.
I am as fast as a cheetah.
S mart at school.

I am a monkey leaping everywhere.
S chool is sweet.

M y mum is kind.
E ager as an eagle.

Dylan Greer (8)
Hob Moor Community Primary School, Acomb

This Is Me

T alented footballer
H appy, helpful, honest
I am a tough cookie
S ophisticated.

I am a bouncy ball
S ocial.

M y name is Jacob, I am jealous
E ager.

Jacob Speck (7)
Hob Moor Community Primary School, Acomb

This Is Me

T alented game-breaker.
H elpful.
I nspirational.
S ocial.

I nteresting.
S leepy.

M eteoric.
E xcitable.

Nicky Howes (8)
Hob Moor Community Primary School, Acomb

All You Need To Know About Me

This is me,
I'm slow when the flow goes,
I'm bright as the sight of light,
I peep when heaps of sheep leap,
I'm scared of heights, that makes me hyper as a fast fighter,
The smell of powder makes me cower when it reminds me of a tint of flower,
I hate being late, that makes me want to faint,
I like staying in bed, that makes me a lazy head,
Liars make me cry, leaving all their words in my precious heart,
Pain will leave me, but words will always stay,
My heart will last forever, but my money will burn in a hot, steaming fire,
My deeds will grow bigger and bigger as time goes.

Laiba Abbas (10)
Rawdhatul Uloom Primary School, Burnley

How To Make An Outstanding Imaan!

To create me, you will need:
Five pieces of stars and books
An inch of mischief and fun
A bucket of kindness and fairness
A sprinkle of puzzles
Ten tons of sleep
Five running cheetahs and three howling wolves.

Now you need to:
1) Add five pieces of stars and books
2) With a mixture of five running cheetahs and three howling wolves
3) With a bucket of kindness and fairness
4) Then stir adding ten tons of sleep
5) An inch of mischief and fun
6) Finally, a sprinkle of puzzles
This is me!

Imaan Fatima (10)
Rawdhatul Uloom Primary School, Burnley

I'm A Muslim!

I'm a Muslim,
The things I say I do every day,
Water, juice and milk, they are the things I drink,
I play and play, I read the Quran too,
I do duaa for everyone, I love to be a Muslim,
Before I eat I say bismillah, after I eat I say alhamdulillah,
I do lots of work at school and I do a page at home,
Worshipping Allah gives good deeds,
Be a very beautiful human for Allah,
Allah has ninety-nine very beautiful names,
Allah created us as beautiful creatures,
I love you, who made us.

Mariah Mirza (7)
Rawdhatul Uloom Primary School, Burnley

My Career

I got a phone call from Arsenal.
I got in my car and travelled quite far.
You know how much petrol that cost?
Just at that moment, I got lost.
I guessed right and went from north to south.
I went to the training ground and did kick-ups.
But before that, I ate too quick and got hiccups.
My heart was burning like fire because of my stamina.
So I made improvements and got better, just like Xhaka!

Just like my dream, being in a football team
And being the next right midfielder.

Adil Ahmed (10)
Rawdhatul Uloom Primary School, Burnley

The Lovely Me

Hi! This is me.
I am free.
I can make tea.
I am fun but bring mischief along.
I sometimes feel a pinch of paint on my tongue.
I play puzzles, games, sometimes painting too.
I am a jewellery wearer.
And a hard worker.
You can give me a challenge.
I'm sure I will crack the code!
Practising nasheeds, that feels just like me.
Cooking and baking, reading books.
Eating chocolate, drawing pictures.
M for me, you should sometimes call me.
Now! You know me!

Maryam Mirza (9)
Rawdhatul Uloom Primary School, Burnley

How To Make A Brilliant Basil!

Ingredients to create me:
100 pounds of speed.
99.9% of jumping.
A spoonful of energy.
A bucket filled with sports.
A room full of braveness.
130 centimetres of height.
A pack full of wolves.

How to create me:
First, grab a bowl the size of a mansion.
Next, add 100 pounds of speed to the bowl.
After that, mix 99.9% of jumping and a spoonful of energy.
Finally, add 130 centimetres of height, a room full of braveness and a pack of wolves!

Basil Yousaf (9)
Rawdhatul Uloom Primary School, Burnley

Astounding Abdul Rahmaan

I am very sporty,
But I'm never naughty!
I try to stay out of trouble,
But I am humble!
I am very healthy,
I like saving up money so I am wealthy.
I like playing cricket,
So I can hit the wicket.
I like playing football,
So I can score a goal.
I like eating pizza,
My favourite animal is a cheetah.
I like blowing balloons,
But would laugh to see baboons!
I can write neater,
But I'm not a veggie eater!
This is me!

Abdul Rahmaan Arslan (9)
Rawdhatul Uloom Primary School, Burnley

Giants

T aller than a house.
H ard and strong like a giant.
I 'm taller than a house but smaller than the world.
S top and make way for the giants or they will crush you.

I really love giants.
S tealing is bad so don't do it or giants will get involved.

M e and my friends are giants that are big and hard.
E ating is what giants love.

My giant's name is Solid.

Ibrahim Shakeel (7)
Rawdhatul Uloom Primary School, Burnley

Perfect Parveen

To create me, you will need:
A cup of beauty
125 grams of fun
A pinch of cuteness
Twenty-five grams of creativity.

Now you need to:
Add a cup of beauty
Stir in twenty-five grams of creativity
Then add 125 grams of fun
And finally add a pinch of cuteness
Now put it in a baking tray
Then bake for fifteen minutes
There you have your perfect Parveen!

Zubaidah Parveen (9)
Rawdhatul Uloom Primary School, Burnley

How To Make Nusaybah

To make me, you will need:
Fifty-five kilograms of smiles
A bowl of glitter
A mix of fun
A pinch of gentleness and politeness
A dash of softness and cuteness.

Now you need to:
Add fifty-five kilograms of smiles
Pour in a huge bowl of glitter
Stir in a pinch of gentleness and politeness
A dash of softness and cuteness
Cook until you can smell cuteness.

Nusaybah Raees (9)
Rawdhatul Uloom Primary School, Burnley

My Favourite Animal Is...

My hedgehog is very pokey,
It went in the water and it was soaky.
It is very sharp
And it likes to play the harp.
It's the colour brown,
It wears a charming, golden crown.
It is very small
And when it is scared it curls up into a ball.
It's tiny,
It's very shiny.
It is very little,
It likes to eat Skittles.

Halimah Mahmood (10)
Rawdhatul Uloom Primary School, Burnley

This Is Me

I'm sweet, gentle and kind!
I really love my family
Me and my family went for a hunt!
I'm very good and I love makeup
Sometimes I eat cakes
I love my life
I like going to school and mosque
And I like to sing a rap, oh yeah
Me and my baby are twins
I love my teacher and my parent
I'm a rap girl, yeah.

Safa Afzal (7)
Rawdhatul Uloom Primary School, Burnley

How To Be Me!

I am a brilliant baker.
I love to eat ice cream.
If you are looking for an artist, just call me.
I am a good person to help, if you need it.
I am a really fast runner and a good sports person.
I've got a good and bright personality.
If you need any help, you can always come to me!
I am an animal lover!
That's me!

Amirah Hussain (9)
Rawdhatul Uloom Primary School, Burnley

I Am A Superstar!

F ans are screaming!
O ver 10,000 people are watching.
O n ground, 100 people are shouting my name.
T en people are wanting me.
B all is banging!
A ll the people are staring.
L ots of people are standing
L ots are enjoying the game.

Muhammad Umar (7)
Rawdhatul Uloom Primary School, Burnley

My Favourite Animal

This animal is as furry as a cat
It's a food craver and loves to eat bamboo sticks
It lives in the cold and has paws sharper than a sword
Whether you like it or not
It's still my favourite animal
Dangerous or not, it's still a cute beast.

What animal am I?

Laiba Bi (10)
Rawdhatul Uloom Primary School, Burnley

Football

I like football.
I score a goal every round.
I am a striker.
I win all around.
I tackle everyone.
I sometimes meg some people.
I can win every day.
I can go there every day.
I go there every Thursday and Wednesday.
I'm going now.
I go there at 10:00.

Talha Ali (7)
Rawdhatul Uloom Primary School, Burnley

Spectacular Sana

I am a healthy eater
And an easy beater
I am a kind talker
And a gentle poker.

Dodgeball is my favourite sport
My teacher is the one who taught.

I am very healthy
My mum gets everything because she's wealthy.

This is me!

Sana Mirza (9)
Rawdhatul Uloom Primary School, Burnley

Aysha Dean

A ysha is amazing,
Y oung and happy,
S mart and clever,
H ard-working,
A lways shy.

D ecorative person,
E xcellent at reading,
A rt lover,
N ever naughty.

This is me!

Aysha Dean (9)
Rawdhatul Uloom Primary School, Burnley

This Is Me

My favourite colour is light pink
I love to drink hot drinks
My favourite animal is a leopard
I hate my food being peppered
I love fashion with a passion
I love Roblox but I hate robots
I'm sweet, I'm nice, but I hate spice
This is me.

Zulekha Parveen (10)
Rawdhatul Uloom Primary School, Burnley

This Is Me! Magnificent Maryam

A kennings poem

This is all about me!
Chocolate eater
Late sleeper
Koala lover
Slow eater
Slow runner
Blue lover
Hard worker
Ice cream eater
Milk drinker
Heavy sleeper
Long talker
School lover
Pineapple eater
This is me!

Maryam Noor (9)
Rawdhatul Uloom Primary School, Burnley

Lipstick

I like lipstick
I am as nice as a butterfly
I am as red as a rose
My name is Matte Me Metallic
My colour is red
My lipstick winds as high as a giraffe
My lid is as gold as the Kabah.

Faatimah Arslan (7)
Rawdhatul Uloom Primary School, Burnley

Cats

I love cats, cats are very fluffy.
Cats are very little.
Cats are very cute.
Cats are very splashy.
Cats are very naughty.
Cats scratch a lot.

But I love cats.

Rayhaan Shaikh (7)
Rawdhatul Uloom Primary School, Burnley

A Natural Skater!

I am a natural skater!
I love my blue skateboard!
I like the red wheels
It takes you on amazing adventures!
Try it for yourself
And see for yourself!

Abudrda Mirza (9)
Rawdhatul Uloom Primary School, Burnley

You Are Unique

I am silly like a goose.
I am different, you are different, that makes us unique.
At times it is sad, but people will make you laugh.
As messy as I am, it does not matter if gay or lesbian, I will be proud no matter what, and all people will.
Like if you are a boy or a girl, it does not make people treat you the same.
If you have brown skin or white skin, you should be proud of yourself.
If you are smart or dumb, it does not matter, just keep trying.
I have brown hair and blue eyes.
People are unique, it does not matter if you are different with different bits, people make you happy.
If you are a tomboy or a boy that wears a dress, lots of people make you happy.
The whole world, people are unique, so you should be happy.

Lilly Deeks (10)
St Margaret's Primary Academy, Lowestoft

A Riddle About What I Love

My head's hurting but I don't mind.
I'm going around, up and down in a circle.
I smell disgusting poop everywhere I go.
I hear animals making noises as well.
I see tons of fences and a brick building.
I always touch the soft animals every time I go.
And the animals are always hungry.
They're a bit fat but that's okay, I still love them the same as I did before.
They're really cute and lovely.
They're really noisy.
They sometimes go to shows and practise at home.
Sometimes they get sick but they always get better.
They can get a bit naughty.
They sometimes hit me with their tail.
Even though they're sometimes bad I still love them.

Lola-Rose Heslop (9)
St Margaret's Primary Academy, Lowestoft

What I Like And What I Like About Myself

I like that I have freckles because not a lot of people have them.
I like football and playing with my best friends.
Harry is sensible, Louis chats all the time, Alfie only listens to his mates and Liam looks out of the window.
I like playing and running around and playing with my mates.
And I like watching football and Top Gear.
I like doing YouTube videos, I've done 257 vids!
I like playing with my dog and practising for football.
I play football with my dog and watch movies with my mum and dad!
I sleep at my grandad's every weekend, I used to have a car.
It was a Citroen Saxo 1.4 and it was my childhood, I loved it.
This is me!

Louis Freeman (10)
St Margaret's Primary Academy, Lowestoft

I Am Cara

I am Cara, I love family and care for everything,
Animals, children and babies
I will be getting a puppy
A black labrador or a cocker spaniel
I am one of the sportiest
I love Norwich City
My favourite food is cod
And my favourite pack up is Chinese
I love rice and I love reborns.
I have five reborns
I have one boy and four girls
I have one reborn called Delitan
And I have had her since I was born, so eight years old
I am half Scottish and half English
I have two ponds
When I do jobs I get five pounds every time I do a job
I have pet fish and I am going to London with my nan and my auntie.

Cara Blevins (8)
St Margaret's Primary Academy, Lowestoft

A Poem About Me

T he thing that makes me happy is when I get time to play with my rabbits and my friends.
H air as long as spaghetti, and as yellow and as shiny as a star.
I like school and my teacher is the best, I really like to learn new things in maths and English.
S ummer is the best because I always like to see the flowers.

I really like to play with Jasmin because she is always kind.
S moothies are my favourite because I get to always make them.

M y favourite foods are ice cream, sushi, strawberries, apples and sweets.
E ating spicy Doritos is my favourite.

Erin Golds (9)
St Margaret's Primary Academy, Lowestoft

Jared's Train Poem

T rains, yes I like trains
R eally like trains, I don't know
A nything I don't like about them
I really like them, they make
N o more pollution, less traffic
S o trains are the best.

T rams came before them
R eally early before, they
A re like trains but have very loud cars
I like trains better than them
N ow the trains can move really fast
S o they are fast

Also, I like subway trains
I like all types of trains
They are all really good
I like trains, they are the best.

Jared Brooks Savage (8)
St Margaret's Primary Academy, Lowestoft

All About Me

A ny flavour, it really doesn't matter, I love Haribo.
L ast Halloween, I was devastated because of Covid.
L ast year, I got a new bed.

A ll animals are guaranteed to be adorable!
B est animal of all has to be a duck!
O n Reverse Time at Pleasure Beach I started screaming!
U ntil next month, I'm going to be celebrating Halloween.
T omorrow is Friday, and that's my favourite day.

M onkeys are very cool animals, they act like humans!
E mus are very big and cute birds.

Dylan Wood (9)
St Margaret's Primary Academy, Lowestoft

All About Me And My Friends And Family

A ll my family love me
L ove my school because it's cool
F ootball's my thing
I love my family and those who love me
E veryone likes my teacher, he's full of funny dad jokes.

H alloween is spooky and full of scary surprises
O liver is short and funny
P umpkins have scary faces
K atie makes me smile all of the time
I like school because I get to see all of my friends
N othing makes me sad or lonely
S ports is my main thing.

Alfie Hopkins (10)
St Margaret's Primary Academy, Lowestoft

My Life

T his is one of my favourite things to do, to write poems with joy.
H ow I love my family, in a great way.
O ctober is the month of Halloween.
M arch is before April, which is my birthday month.
A s a kid, life is great.
S weet and sour foods are yummy and not yucky.

S peedy and strong isn't my thing.
A kitten is the cutest thing.
M y favourite food is spaghetti.
U FOs seem really cool.
E aster has lots of chocolate.
L ove is life.

Thomas Shackleton (9)
St Margaret's Primary Academy, Lowestoft

This Is Me!

I like doughnuts because they are a circle
I like dragon games because you can ride them
I like penguins because they do the paddle walk
I like Halloween because I can scare people
I like fruit because it is healthy
I like Spain because it is sunny
I like swimming because I can jump in
I like cake because it is chocolate
I like money because I can buy stuff
I like apples because they are juicy
I like grapes
I like strawberries
I like my family
I like blackcurrant juice
I like Christmas.

Cohen Kirk (8)
St Margaret's Primary Academy, Lowestoft

My Dreams, Personality And Favourite Things

Dreams:
I wish I was half-dragon and had a pet baby ice dragon.
I wish that I was as strong as an earthquake and as fast as a tidal wave.
I wish I was an Airbender.
I wish I was as tough as titanium.

Personality:
I like sports and drawing.
Riding my bike and playing my Xbox.
I can be calm or very angry, stubborn.

Favourite things:
My family, dodgeball, playing Grounded, Fortnite, Roblox, Ark
My friends, my dog, eating, dinosaurs, alligators, huskies
And playtime with Mum and Dad.

Tommy Buckle (8)
St Margaret's Primary Academy, Lowestoft

I Am Me

I am me
I live by the sea
My name is Zoe
And I like to be me.

I'm not very tall
But I like to be small
Like the fish in the sea
Who swim in the sea happily.

I like to draw
And paint on the floor
And dance in my bedroom
To my favourite tune.

When it's time for brunch
I have a packed lunch
With my brothers sitting beside me.

I like animals
Furry and scaly
Animals are lovely
Of every kind
And I never leave a heart behind.

Zoe Morris (8)
St Margaret's Primary Academy, Lowestoft

I Love London

When I woke up, my dad said, "We are going to London!"
I danced with happiness, crying and said, "Wow!"
So I leapt out of bed and I sprinted down the steep stairs,
Got breakfast and I ate all of it,
Then I sprinted back upstairs, brushed my teeth, washed my face, and then I got dressed.
I sprinted down the steep stairs, put on my shoes, rushed out the door, got in the car and said, "London we're coming!"
I am so excited, we arrived at London and we saw Matilda and went home.

Lois
St Margaret's Primary Academy, Lowestoft

Who I Am

I am a great gamer.
I am silly most of the time.
I am a fan of spooky stuff.
I am ten years old.
I am very lucky to have my happy family.
I am a fast dude.
I am very funny.
I am a big fan of the colours black and red.
I am very happy most of the time, but do get sad sometimes.
I am over-excited to have a lovely, cute sister, sometimes annoying or naughty, and her name is Isla.
I am a person that has a problem with sleeping.
I am very good at maths.

Finley Wilton (10)
St Margaret's Primary Academy, Lowestoft

This Football

I am a footballer, I like Cristano Ronaldo
I am a footballer,
My name is Logan W,
I am a fast footballer,
My friend thinks I am like Neymar,
I'm good at maths,
I'm a joker,
I'm a striker,
A funny joker,
A funny footballer,
A funny fast footballer,
I've got the best football skills.
I love my family,
They are the best mum and dad ever!
My dad, is the best dad ever,
He is the best footballer ever in the world!

Logan Winyard (9)
St Margaret's Primary Academy, Lowestoft

This Is Me!

J umping is my favourite action
O n my hyper stage, mostly
S aturdays are the best
E asy English is the quickest subject
P lease is a word I don't use much, that I should
H appy is an expression I mostly show.

K ind sometimes
N ever weep
I love McDonald's
G etting sour sweets all of the time
H igh fives to my BFF all of the time
T aylor is a good friend.

Joseph Knight (9)
St Margaret's Primary Academy, Lowestoft

My Name Is Jemima

I am a girl, but not any girl, I am Jemima
I am quite little and I have short, brown, soft hair
I am special
I am Jemima, I am one of the shortest in my class
I am special
I am Jemima, I am happy with who I meet, what I get to do and how I act
I would never change it for the world
I am special
I am Jemima, I am a positive young girl
I am special
I am a girl, but not any girl... I am Jemima!
Be proud of yourself, never beat yourself up.

Jemima Pomfrett (8)
St Margaret's Primary Academy, Lowestoft

Me

My name is Finlay and I am nine years old
And when I grow up I want to be a policeman.
My name is Finlay and I am nine years old
And I like playing with Lego with my brother, I love to build things.
My name is Finlay and I am nine years old
And I have lots of pets, one dog, two cats and eight rats and I love them so much.
My name is Finlay and I am nine years old
And I live with my mummy and daddy and my little brother, Luca, and little sister, Tilly.

Finlay-Jack Page (9)
St Margaret's Primary Academy, Lowestoft

All About Daisy

D islike celery
A lways joyful
I love my friends and family
S weets are better than peas
Y ou'll always see me eating dessert.

My teacher is the best one I have ever had.
My teacher is amazing and nice and also really kind.
My favourite subject is computing and maths.
I mostly wear dresses.
My favourite animals are kittens.
My hair is brown as Nutella.
I love going to the beach and school.

Daisy McLelland (9)
St Margaret's Primary Academy, Lowestoft

The Pendolino

The Pendolino's pantograph roars as it tilts and turns around the corners of the track at one hundred and twenty miles per hour.
Blasting to a stop, it opens its doors to welcome its passengers on board this Avanti West Coast Pendolino service.
Then the throttle is full-powered, and the Pendolino zooms into the distance.
Then the train explodes through Rugby, going *zoom, zoom, zoom, zoom!*
Then it speeds up more and more, away and away and away.

Junior Hayden-Hindes (10)
St Margaret's Primary Academy, Lowestoft

My Life

M y favourite thing is Harry Potter.
I am a book reader and an awesome gamer.
L ife can get me down but I try my best.
A wesome at maths and a Harry Potter reader.
S ometimes moody, but mostly happy.

L ife is fun when I'm with my friends.
I am a Ravenclaw from Harry Potter.
F ar and wide across the world, I meet new people.
E arly in the morning I watch Harry Potter.

Mila Lubbock (9)
St Margaret's Primary Academy, Lowestoft

I Am Who I Want To Be

I love to play football, I started when I was six.

A s a pupil of a very nice school, whenever I find learning boring, I make fun out of it.

M y family members are my favourite people in the world.

M y friends are the people that would help me at school if I was sad.

E very time I feel sad, I listen to calm music.

I love playing video games.

Life can be hard but I will never give up.

Kayla Louise (9)
St Margaret's Primary Academy, Lowestoft

This Is All About Me

How to create me, you will need:
Ten marshmallows
And one purple colour
And some toys
Some calm
And some bunnies to keep me happy
My eyes are as green as the grass
And I am as happy as the clouds
And I am as happy forever and ever like the sun
I am as fast as a cheetah
All the things I love
I like flowers
The flowers look like bluebells
My love will give you pride and joy
I will give you all my love.

Kaitie-Jade Stockley (7)
St Margaret's Primary Academy, Lowestoft

This Is Me

T hink as fast as a cheetah
H istory is one of my favourites because of learning about the Vikings
I am me and I forever will be
S uper fun to play with, especially in football.

I love hot, cheesy pizza
S cience is one of my favourite subjects because we make things.

M aths is really fun to do, I like subtracting
E nglish is my favourite subject because I like writing.

Henley Brown (9)
St Margaret's Primary Academy, Lowestoft

What I Like

Cats are small, dogs are rough, but bugs are fast as the past.
I like to game, others don't, and that's alright because it's fine.
I have to work, day by day, while others are home away.
I like to grow, I like to eat, and I like to sleep when I'm clean.
My friends are kind, they like to play, but sometimes they are home away.
I'm getting something for November the 10th, it's small and quiet and it likes the dark.

Noah McCondochie (9)
St Margaret's Primary Academy, Lowestoft

Basketball, Snow And Me

A lways up for Oreos
L eft or right, I don't know the way to the park
F unny and kind, that is me
I 'm the best basketball player
E ven smarter than my own mum.

M y mum I love so, so much
C lumsy and crazy
I love the park so, so much
V olume up so I can't hear my sisters
O h yes, it is snowing
R eading is what makes me happy.

Alfie McIvor (9)
St Margaret's Primary Academy, Lowestoft

Happy Always

H orses are my favourite animal
A lways eat broccoli
P ositive all the time
P erhaps a bit angry
Y oung, but I am strong.

A lways up for a challenge
L ove my family, especially my guinea pig
W ednesday is my favourite day
A s short as a mouse
Y ou might think I'm quiet
S ometimes I'm sad, but I'm mostly happy.

Nell Hickinbotham (10)
St Margaret's Primary Academy, Lowestoft

This Is Me

Listen carefully, because this is a poem all about me,
My cat claws crazily,
I am as crazy as a zoo,
I love to sing and dance, what about you?
Don't leave cake unattended because when you come back, it will no longer be there,
I have long, brown hair,
I have a dog, she loves to play and sleep,
I love animals, my fave are pandas,
If I could have white chocolate every day I would,
And that is me!

Imogen Allison (10)
St Margaret's Primary Academy, Lowestoft

All About Me

M y favourite teacher is Miss Gayler,
A lways eating hot dogs, but my mum never buys them,
D ashing with my only budgie, its name is Tearry
D ancing for an hour every Wednesday,
I love to eat Oreos as well,
S easide is my favourite place to be,
O n my bed eating Flamin' Hot Cheetos,
N utella is my favourite thing to put on toast.

This is me!

Maddison Hopkins (9)
St Margaret's Primary Academy, Lowestoft

To Create Me You Will Need

A lot of fruits and vegetables
A shelf of books
Five litres of melted chocolate
A pinch of fun and mischief
A dash of happiness and sadness
A sprinkle of darkness
A slab of trifle.

Now you need to:
Add a lot of fruits and vegetables
And a shelf a books
Five litres of melted chocolate
A pinch of fun and mischief
A dash of happiness and sadness
And mix a trifle.

Daisy-Rae Taylor (9)
St Margaret's Primary Academy, Lowestoft

Halloween And What I Am

I am a Halloween lover but I don't dress up
I wear a hoodie with something that's from Halloween
Like a ghost or pumpkin.
About spiders, they have a thousand eyes and eight legs
And make sticky white webs.
I am a girl with brown, short hair with a fringe.
I am a dragon book collector, anything with dragons.
I like huskies and Saint Bernards.
I make cushions and loads of other stuff.

Maisy Clements (8)
St Margaret's Primary Academy, Lowestoft

Football

I am the best goalie on my team.
I am a really good striker in football.
I am the best when I put on my football shoes.
I am faster than lightning when I play football in my shoes.
I am friends with Henley and Jack and big man Dalton and they love football, just like me.
I am training my football skills in my garden, that is so good.
I win all the time.
I am the best football player in my team.

Kyle Charlton (9)
St Margaret's Primary Academy, Lowestoft

This Is Me

My family is the best because they are helpful and they are funny
They make me laugh when I laugh.
I love to help but sometimes it isn't the right time
Because I might be moody or angry with my sisters or brothers.
When I go swimming it might be scary
Because you might jump in the deep end.
I like music, but not too loud.
I want to be a vet because I love to help, and love animals.

Poppie Nash (8)
St Margaret's Primary Academy, Lowestoft

This Is Me!

I am Mary-Jane
My hair is blonde
My eyes are brown
I have loads of freckles
My favourite colour is a dark purple
I do gymnastics on a Thursday
And dance on Wednesday
My favourite animals are pandas, rabbits and cats
My cats are called Rusty, Patchey, Scampy and Galaxy
I love to sleep
My favourite food is pizza
I have an annoying brother
This is all about me!

Mary-Jane Grammage (10)
St Margaret's Primary Academy, Lowestoft

My Favourite Sport

Football's my thing
England made it to the Euro final
And I'm proud
I support Liverpool all day long
After God accidentally made me run too fast
The war between Messi and Ronaldo is still going
I have to agree, it's Ronaldo
I've been training to be a goalkeeper
And soon I'll be better than Neuer
This was me, about me being sporty.

Fynley Dowler (10)
St Margaret's Primary Academy, Lowestoft

My Life

H alloween is spooky!
A lso my life is amazing.
L ions are cute!
L ove is everything.
U sually summer is lots of fun!
M um is the best.
S cootering can hurt me sometimes.

L ove my dog.
I enjoy gaming.
F un is an amazing feeling.
E veryone thinks I'm a good friend!

Hallum Magee (10)
St Margaret's Primary Academy, Lowestoft

Christmas

- **C** hoccies
- **H** azelnuts
- **R** eindeer
- **I** ce
- **S** anta
- **T** insel
- **M** ollie
- **A** nts
- **S** isters

Don't you think Halloween and Christmas are the best?
If you don't, well try it
You can buy the costumes
Spooky and the Christmas ones are fantastic
Try them on now, quick, go go go.

Mollie Shaw (8)
St Margaret's Primary Academy, Lowestoft

Describe Myself

I love cats.
I am a kind friend.
I can run as fast as a cheetah.
I like ice cream.
I like pizza.
I like candyfloss.
I like popcorn.
I like cupcakes.
I make funny jokes.
I like my teachers.
I like chocolate.
I like to eat candy.
I'm a cookie maker.
I have brown eyes like a muddy pool.
I like parties with my friends.

Tiffany Rogers (7)
St Margaret's Primary Academy, Lowestoft

This Is Me!

My favourite animal...

G orgeous animal and better than the rest
I solated in a zoo, but people love them
R obot-like because they don't move much
A wesome at being adorable, no matter what
F antastic at amusing people
F abulous entertainers with anything
E legant, but sometimes clumsy.

Eavan White (9)
St Margaret's Primary Academy, Lowestoft

This Is Me

I'm a very sporty child.
I am a football fanatic.
My favourite food is pizza and ice cream.
I'm really kind and a bit mischievous.
I love my family and we are holidaymakers and it's very fun.
I play with my friends a lot.
My favourite colour is red.
I have two dogs, two naughty dogs
As naughty as Elf on the Shelf.

Parker Jeffs (7)
St Margaret's Primary Academy, Lowestoft

Facts About Me!

I'm awesome, kind, silly, curious and sporty.
I like dancing, jumping, leaping, running and I work a lot on basketball.
I want to be a builder to give homeless people homes.
Football is my thing, I support Liverpool all year long
And soon I'll be better than ever.
I do tag, rugby, football, tennis and I like playing video games.

Aden Moyse (10)
St Margaret's Primary Academy, Lowestoft

My Life Story

I have a cat called Dora
I have a rat called Scabbers
When I was a baby my heart wouldn't grow
It had a gap and I went to the hospital
And then my heart was here again
When I was four years old my heart was not here again
They did surgery and I'm all here again
And I'm at school and I'm in Year Three now.

Isabella Smith (7)
St Margaret's Primary Academy, Lowestoft

This Is Me!

My hair is brown, I like my town
I like to dance and to play with my friends
I like to sing songs, but when it has to end I get sad
But hopefully it will all start again
And when it starts it will be better than ever.

My sisters are annoying but I like them anyway
But when they anger me I really have to say go away.

Tilley Beresford (11)
St Margaret's Primary Academy, Lowestoft

This Is Me

I am a helper.
I am a cook.
I am a camper.
I love my family.
I like red lobsters.
My hair is brown like chocolate.
I have lots of friends.
I have a BFF, best friends forever.
I have a lovely teacher.
I love reading.
My family is kind.
I like having fun.
I am kind.
I don't have pets.

Lacey McIvor (7)
St Margaret's Primary Academy, Lowestoft

About Me!

Sitting down, the screen turns on.
My controller clicks again and again.
The TV moves as I click.
Now the TV starts to make vicious, deadly noises like a bomb.
Then minutes later people cheer, like someone screaming at me.
Then I leave to get to the selection of fun and amazing games.
Now I can ready up to get in a game.

Tyler Hutcheson (9)
St Margaret's Primary Academy, Lowestoft

Love Is Life

L ove is life
O ther things rule too!
V alentine's is the best
E verything is the best.

I llness is horrible
S weets are good, so am I.

L ive your life, feel happy
I love everything
F orest School is the best
E verything rules.

Taylor Louch (9)
St Margaret's Primary Academy, Lowestoft

This Is Me!

I love to dance all day long
But travelling is the best
So I can see new places.

This is me!

I love cats
They are cute and nature is amazing
I love to go outdoors.

This is me!

Chocolate is amazing
But I don't like fruit
Because chocolate rules and fruit drools.

Holly Dyer (8)
St Margaret's Primary Academy, Lowestoft

My Best Features

Wavy hair and faint freckles,
These are my best features,
One eye white, orange and blue,
Which makes me look like a cat and an eagle,
The other brown and green,
As weird as a monkey,
I climb the trees,
Animal lover and deep sleeper,
Whenever I'm down my friends bring me up.

This is me!

Eve-Louise Chapman (11)
St Margaret's Primary Academy, Lowestoft

The Facts About Me!

This is my hobby, I ain't called Bobby.
I'm fearless, I'm chilled, I ain't thrilled!
I'm fun, I don't have a son.
I ain't lonely, I do roly-polies.
I like scootering, I don't like going in the root of it.
I like doing tricks, they're quite hard, but I think I can get through it!

Scott Ardley (10)
St Margaret's Primary Academy, Lowestoft

What Makes Me Happy

R ock and roll is my jam.
Y um Yums are my favourite food.
A nd they should be yours too.
N eptune is a pretty cool planet.

A pples are juicy.
R iddles make me giggle.
L avender smells nice.
O ranges I dislike.
W inning makes me happy.

Ryan Arlow (9)
St Margaret's Primary Academy, Lowestoft

Daniella

D ogs and cats are my favourite
A lways hyper
N ice and sweet at home
I love Oreos and gummy bears
E lves are my favourite because they make a mess for me to play with
L ove annoying my sister
L ove my best friend
A lways playing with my best friend.

Daniella Pasquale (9)
St Margaret's Primary Academy, Lowestoft

I'm A Lightning Bolt, Going Through The Sky At The Speed Of Light

I've got a meteor in my fist
I am a football player
I'm a millionaire
I'm a BBQ ribs lover
I like Harry Kane
I like Fortnite
I like David Walliams
I like juice
I like grapes
I like red
I like Son of Arugal
I like doing a backflip
I like hugs
I love biking.

Connor Hopkins (9)
St Margaret's Primary Academy, Lowestoft

All About Me

I like to dance but not to prance.
I go to gym but not to win.
I have lots of fun when I'm with my friends,
But not when it all has to end.
I love chocolate, it tastes so good,
But sweets, I never could.
I love my sisters so, so much
And I also love when they make me lunch.

Clara Westgate (10)
St Margaret's Primary Academy, Lowestoft

I Love My Family And Friends

F amily is important to me.
R eading is so fun and good to learn.
I ce is cold to eat.
E nd of 'The Neverending Story' is my favourite story.
N its, I don't like nits okay.
D oughnuts, I love doughnuts.
S lime, I like slime I do.

Ellah-Maye Serina Johnston (9)
St Margaret's Primary Academy, Lowestoft

Oscar Cushion

O range is my favourite colour
S pace lover
C hocolate lover
A pple lover
R esilient.

C urly hair
U nusual
S uper weird
H elpful
I ncredible
O scar is my name
N ever mean.

Oscar Cushion (9)
St Margaret's Primary Academy, Lowestoft

This Is Me!

I am as happy as The Loud House when they move to Scotland.
I am as clever as a teacher.
I am really excited when I go to the park.
I love my family when they laugh, but I love them anyway.
I am a cream lover.
My hair is as soft as a fluffy sheep, my hair is as yellow as the sun.

Alivia Dixon
St Margaret's Primary Academy, Lowestoft

Me And My School

T he world is a dream.
H ave eyes as brown as the dirt.
I t's lovely having a pet.
S ee friendship forever.

I s the best to be in this class.
S he has everything.

M ischief boy.
E verything is the best.

Lennie Hodges (7)
St Margaret's Primary Academy, Lowestoft

This Is Me!

I am an Islam person and I am eight years old.
I love food and swimming and I am a panda.
Well, I wish I was.
My favourite animals are koalas, pandas and cats.
I like watching My Hero and Naruto.
My favourite games are Mario Kart, Naruto and My Hero
And I like baking.

Eeridesu Cetin (8)
St Margaret's Primary Academy, Lowestoft

My Life Is Good

I have friends
My favourite part of school is afternoon
People think I am different to them
Some think I am bad at everything
I love my dog, I love my family
I love dogs and cats, I love to sleep
I like my teacher Mr Ferry
I love Star Wars
I love Italy.

Levi Stanborough (10)
St Margaret's Primary Academy, Lowestoft

Football

F rankie is my name
O ctopus is my favourite sea creature
O ranges are my favourite fruit
T igers are my favourite animal
B eans are my favourite food
A lways playing with my dog
L ike football
L ove football.

Frankie Yeo (8)
St Margaret's Primary Academy, Lowestoft

Who Is She?

Lilly is fluffy and soft,
When I come home she jumps up at me and licks me,
Sometimes she scratches me but I do not mind because she is cute,
When I sit down she gets on the sofa and sits on me, or next to me,
When I go out somewhere she sits at the door and waits for me.

Scarlett Lee-Hagger (9)
St Margaret's Primary Academy, Lowestoft

I Am Me

I like to sing as loud as I can, but not too loud.
I sing like a professional singer.
I love to sing, it's my thing.
It's like a hobby and I do it a lot, to be honest with you.
I am an amazing swimmer because I like the water.
My daddy taught me how to swim.

Isabelle Girling (8)
St Margaret's Primary Academy, Lowestoft

This Is Me!

I am as kind as a friend.
I am as nice as my family.
I am as loved as my mum.
I like to play in the park.
I love my mum.
I like to eat fruit and vegetables.
I love lots of apples.
I always like to play with Millie.
I always like to play with Lucia.

Teesha Liburd (7)
St Margaret's Primary Academy, Lowestoft

I Am Faith

F riendly
A lways helpful
I love popcorn
T rick or treat?
H igh energy.

P et hamster
E ats candy
A ll about books
R eally love gymnastics
C hristian
E ats carrots.

Faith Pearce (8)
St Margaret's Primary Academy, Lowestoft

Charlie

C hocolate is my favourite food
H appiness is reading 'Goosebumps'
A football always keeps me happy
R abbits are my favourite animal
L ove stuff I find
I love my baby sis
E mily is my least favourite sis.

Charlie Reeves
St Margaret's Primary Academy, Lowestoft

I Am A Twin

I am a twin.

A lice is my name
M y sister looks like me.

A wesome I am.

T rouble when we are together
W e are a great team
I wear glasses, so does she
N ow this is me!

Alice Burbridge (10)
St Margaret's Primary Academy, Lowestoft

This Is Me!

Ellie, that is me,
I want to play football professionally,
I run fast as a hare,
When I'm sad, my friends are always there,
My favourite bird is a woodpecker,
I will always miss Mr Fletcher,
The number seventeen is lucky,
That was me.

Ellie Davies (11)
St Margaret's Primary Academy, Lowestoft

I Am Awesome

I am a book reader
I am a gamer
I am an Eddie Stobart finder
I am a Ferrari, Lamborghini and Bugatti finder
I wish I was rich
I wish I was on Top Gear
I like The Simpsons
I like Underdog
And finally
Go-kart lover.

Logan Caulkin (9)
St Margaret's Primary Academy, Lowestoft

This Is Me

B lue eyes
R eally good reader
O range is my favourite colour
O ranges are orange and one of my favourites
K ind
E gg is my favourite food.

This poem is about me
I am Brooke-Leigh.

Brooke-Leigh Layton (7)
St Margaret's Primary Academy, Lowestoft

All About Me!

J umpy
A lways kind
S heep are my favourite, they're so fluffy
M y favourite colour is red, it's very bright
I believe my sister is the best but annoying sometimes
N ever unkind to anyone.

Jasmin Walpole (10)
St Margaret's Primary Academy, Lowestoft

All About Me

I feel happy when I'm with my dog.
When I'm sleepy I go to sleep.
I have ocean-like eyes, they shimmer in the day and night.
I love to eat fruit, it's my favourite snack to eat.
I love maths, it's my favourite lesson.

Lucy Stammers (10)
St Margaret's Primary Academy, Lowestoft

The Barking Of My House

As I walk through the door
You can hear loud steps and barking
As I get pushed on the sofa I'm laughing in excitement
As they sit on me with their fluff, laying on me
And I love when I go to sleep
They'll lay on my lap.

Roman Morris (9)
St Margaret's Primary Academy, Lowestoft

What You Need To Make Me

A cup of mischief
Lots of pizza
A comfy bed to sleep on every day
Long, blonde hair
With crystal-blue eyes
I am a lightning bolt in football boots
I am an excellent striker
A kindness giver
A happiness bringer.

Shane Gibbs (10)
St Margaret's Primary Academy, Lowestoft

What I Love

I like to bake.
My favourite food is cookies.
I have lots of family members.
I have three dogs.
I have a very nice teacher.
My eyes are as green as grass.
My lips are as red as a rose.
I've got lots of friends.

Kasey-Ann Nwaefuna (8)
St Margaret's Primary Academy, Lowestoft

This Is Me

I started when I was young
Kicking the ball around the house
I wanted to go pro in football
People doubted me every day
I got into a team
And showed everyone wrong
I'm now on the way to play pro
This is me.

Ethan Hemsley (11)
St Margaret's Primary Academy, Lowestoft

What Am I?

I like to do the dishes and help my mum when she is poorly.
I like to read books.
I like competitions.
I keep lots of secrets.
I am very good at ventriloquising (my favourite is Benson).

Answer: I am Tom.

Thomas Copeman (9)
St Margaret's Primary Academy, Lowestoft

Poetry Day

Sometimes I may be happy, sad, excited or angry,
but that does not stop me from being me.
Being different is normal, it is just me.
I love dragons, I have a toy dragon at home.
When I grow up I will live beside my family.

Lola Nash (8)
St Margaret's Primary Academy, Lowestoft

This Is Who I Am

I love animals, mostly frogs, lizards and fish
I have a pet African land snail, I feed him every week.
I like fish, frogs and lizards because my favourite colours are red, blue and green.
I love my friends and family too.

Myles Lloyd (7)
St Margaret's Primary Academy, Lowestoft

My Puppy

My dog is cute
My dog has very cute eyes
My dog likes eating the toilet paper
He's a small sausage
Well, to say he's brown and black like a burnt sausage
He is always stealing my sock
He is my dog.

Riley Hayden Hindes (8)
St Margaret's Primary Academy, Lowestoft

This Is Me

I box for joy,
My protein shakes keep me alive,
My phone is as old as a male croc,
My dog is a great swimmer,
After that I give her dinner,
I am a great rugby player,
Dad says I have a lot of strength.

Daniel Gadney (11)
St Margaret's Primary Academy, Lowestoft

How I Came To Be

I am the best at making things,
Using items from the past,
Usually a costume,
But they rarely ever last,
My hair is as brown as chocolate,
My eyes are as blue as water.

And this is how I am me!

Kieren Bollans (10)
St Margaret's Primary Academy, Lowestoft

Lottie

L oves to annoy my sister.
O reos make me happy.
T illey makes me angry.
T rying to beat up always.
I love my bunny so so much.
E ating McDonald's is my favourite.

Lottie Beresford (9)
St Margaret's Primary Academy, Lowestoft

Halloween

H appy and exciting
A ll the sweets!
L ove seeing friends
L ove seeing family
O wn sweets
W inter
E at sweets
E at popcorn
N ovember.

Amelia-Lloyd Lloyd (8)
St Margaret's Primary Academy, Lowestoft

Me!

I like to bake
Anything but cake
I like to game
Which may grant me fame
I like to play my guitar
But not when I have to travel far
I love everything about myself
I wouldn't change a thing!

Jacob Bale (10)
St Margaret's Primary Academy, Lowestoft

This Is Me
A kennings poem

I am a...
Footballer
Striker
Mathematician!
Tennis man
Light sleeper
Free kick taker
Chocolate eater
Lovely person
Summer wisher
A joker
And finally I'm a good helper.

Dalton Welton (10)
St Margaret's Primary Academy, Lowestoft

All About Me

I love tigers
I love ice cream
I love little babies
I love lasagne
I love yoghurt
I love sloths
I love hats
I love awesomeness
I love waffle
I love my family
I love my life.

Tilly (10)
St Margaret's Primary Academy, Lowestoft

Halloween Is The Best

H airy spiders
A ncient wizards
L ittle monsters
L ots of candy
O gres
W itches
E normous pumpkins
E pic costumes
N ightmares.

Owen Smith (8)
St Margaret's Primary Academy, Lowestoft

This Is Me And How I Came To Be

I like food and TV too.
My favourite food is McDonald's.
My favourite animals are snakes.
I like dogs, cats and geckos too.
My eyes are an explosion of hazel.
My hair is golden like the sun.

Mason Clemens (10)
St Margaret's Primary Academy, Lowestoft

Coming Home

The door closes, relief,
My bed warmth,
My wallpaper colourful,
My lamp gleaming,
My bookshelf standing,
My cats, meowing, trying to talk,
"Where have you been?" they say.

Scarlett Griffin (9)
St Margaret's Primary Academy, Lowestoft

This Is Me

I am good at gaming, I do it every day
My hair is as dark as midnight
My eyes are an explosion of colours
My favourite colour is green
I am a lion on the inside
But kind and helpful too.

Hayden Kirk (10)
St Margaret's Primary Academy, Lowestoft

This Is Me!

To create me, you must have:

Spicy food
A pinch of mischief
A small room
An animal to chill with
A pillow fort
To be alone.

Then you make me!
This is me!

Rhian Majoram (10)
St Margaret's Primary Academy, Lowestoft

My Life Only

My hair is gold
My skin is smooth
My run is slow
But I have fun anyway
I like to dance and sing songs
I love to play with my black and brown dog
My adventure will never end.

Leah Grimmette (10)
St Margaret's Primary Academy, Lowestoft

This Is Me!

I sassily strut down the catwalk,
I tap quickly,
I think I can do it,
And I can do it!
I gracefully skip around the room,
Wearing tight, pink shoes.
I feel like myself here.

Mia Wright (10)
St Margaret's Primary Academy, Lowestoft

This Is Me

S uper awesome
T he smartest student in the class
E xtremely happy
P erfect
H as a big brain
A superstar
N ice to friends.

Stephan Ferreira
St Margaret's Primary Academy, Lowestoft

This Is Me!
A kennings poem

I am a
Book reader
Wasp flyer
Football watcher
Christmas wisher
Chocolate eater
Late riser
Cake maker
Light sleeper
And finally...
A pro gamer.

Gracie Bloomfield (9)
St Margaret's Primary Academy, Lowestoft

This Is Me, Aslan!

I am as strong as a lion,
Smart as a parrot
And also fantastic at swimming
And proud to be Turkish!
I am also excited when it comes to playing
And always friendly.

Aslan Cetin (10)
St Margaret's Primary Academy, Lowestoft

Me

A kennings poem

I am an...
Amazing dancer
Humour giver
Kindness provider
Red lover
Super sister (to an annoying brother!)
Long hair wearer
Early waker
This is me!

Malaja White (10)
St Margaret's Primary Academy, Lowestoft

Happy

My fave colour is blue
I am a singer and dancer
I love playing with my friends
I love maths
I love going to Norwich and Yarmouth
And I love annoying my grandad.

Roxy Porter (8)
St Margaret's Primary Academy, Lowestoft

This Is Me
A kennings poem

I am an awesome ballet kid.
I am a sweet lover.
I am a deep sleeper.
I am a football lover.
I am a maths lover.
I am a school lover.
I am a teacher lover.

Ellie Potter (7)
St Margaret's Primary Academy, Lowestoft

I Am Bailey Blowers

I like to play with my friends because happy me.
I like my family because happy me.
I like maths best.
But I love my hamster, he is the best.
Happy me.

Bailey Blowers (8)
St Margaret's Primary Academy, Lowestoft

This Is Me!

I have a brother
I have a sister
I have black hair
I like singing
I like dancing
We like dinosaurs
We like ice cream cake.

Lilly Burbridge (10)
St Margaret's Primary Academy, Lowestoft

Barbie

B e you
A ct like you
R euse you
B e cool
I ndependently
E at cake and sweets.

Samantha Macpherson (8)
St Margaret's Primary Academy, Lowestoft

This Is Me!

I am...
As happy as a cheeky monkey,
Funny as a clown,
A curious reader,
An eating lover,
A game lover.

Kal Davidson (8)
St Margaret's Primary Academy, Lowestoft

This Is Me

I am happy to be me and I love my family
I am proud to be me
I love my life
I play with my family and friends.

Rihann Forder
St Margaret's Primary Academy, Lowestoft

Paige

P erfect baker
A wesome reader
I love my mum
G ood reader
E xcited baker.

Paige Louch (6)
St Margaret's Primary Academy, Lowestoft

What Am I?

I am cheeky
I love bananas
I climb trees
I am annoying
I am funny.

Answer: Monkey.

Grace Copeman (7)
St Margaret's Primary Academy, Lowestoft

This Is Me

When I grow up I want to be...
Shiny as a vet
And I want to be a sea swimmer
And a loving teacher.

Gohul (7)
St Margaret's Primary Academy, Lowestoft

I Am Emily

I like pancakes.
I like wolves.
I like friends.
But I love family.
I am a lovely girl.

Emily Smith (8)
St Margaret's Primary Academy, Lowestoft

I Am Holly

I like foxes and wolves
I like unicorns
I like pancakes
But I love family.

Holly Ellen Ralph (8)
St Margaret's Primary Academy, Lowestoft

This Is Me

A kennings poem

Wolf lover
Bunny petter
Dog hugger
Water drinker
Coffee spitter
Friend player
Sassy talker
School learner
Energetic runner
Lazy napper
Short hair disguster
Wasp hater
Scorpion stamper
Bang blower
Fast stopper
Mushroom thrower
Blood orange licker
Family kisser
Tall hater
Long nail hater.

Imogen Cowan (7)
Tickton CE Primary School, Tickton

This Is Me!
A kennings poem

Horse rider
Ticklish screamer
Fringe mover
Lazy sleeper
Small dodger
Kind hugger
Scab picker
Happy eater
Voice croaker
Mud splodger
Drawing hater
Games player
Walk slower
Friendly smiler
Funny joker
Spider crawler
Colouring disposer
Family lover
Bunny speeder
Wolf hunter.

Thea Parker (7)
Tickton CE Primary School, Tickton

This Is Me!
A kennings poem

Snake avoider
Long hair brusher
Fun carer
Mushroom disliker
Spider detester
Crazy dancer
Tomato expeller
Pizza eater
Sprouts hater
Quiet learner
Cat lover
Violin liker
Sports player
Dark runner
Harry Potter reader
Music singer
Classroom tidier
Dark worrier.

Florence Fawke (9)
Tickton CE Primary School, Tickton

This Is Me!
A kennings poem

Animal lover
Allergy hater
Birthday liker
Christmas adorer
Snake escaper
Friend protector
Spider disliker
Sports player
Wobbly things avoider
Skittles eater
Wasp hater
Cheek giver
Intolerance detester
Happiness provider.

Esmay Martin (8)
Tickton CE Primary School, Tickton

This Is Me!
A kennings poem

Wild dancer
Mess maker
Harry Potter reader
Friend protector
Animal lover
Animal carer
Dog walker
Trainer wearer
Sweet sneaker
Wasp avoider
Hot dog disliker
Gymnastics hater
Snot escaper
Gap hater
Cheese hater.

Eva Fisher (8)
Tickton CE Primary School, Tickton

This Is Me!
A kennings poem

Lego lover
McDonald's eater
Funny giggler
Silly lover
Movie watcher
Hot chocolate drinker
Writhing wriggler
Hard chicken hater
Friendly smiler
Creepy doll despiser
Lovely hugger
Titanoboa cheater
Asthmatic wheezer.

Ewan Pottage (7)
Tickton CE Primary School, Tickton

This Is Me

A kennings poem

Buddy friendly
Silly giggler
Rabbit cuddler
Snake hater
Unkind people despiser
Lazy sleeper
Chocolate eater
Beach lover
Snow dancer
Grumpy walker
Happy player
Spider worrier
Wasp screamer
Legs jogger.

Abigail Hadfield (8)
Tickton CE Primary School, Tickton

This Is Me!
A kennings poem

Family lover
Horse rider
Water splasher
Sun layer
Cat scratcher
Hot chocolate spitter
Mud splodger
Rain hider
Funny joker
Kind player
Beautiful dresser
Happy smiler
Fringe hater
Big buyer.

Molly Harrison (7)
Tickton CE Primary School, Tickton

This Is Me

A kennings poem

Friendly hugger
Energetic runner
Silly eater
Playful player
Ice hardener
Dog admirer
Polar bear lover
Sister
Blackcurrant destroyer
Science hater
Spider killer
Wasp stinger
Blister runawayer.

Lucy Harling (7)
Tickton CE Primary School, Tickton

This Is Me!
A kennings poem

Birthday liker
Bee escaper
Big-mouthed learner
Cauliflower disliker
Film watcher
Halloween lover
Hot chocolate drinker
Happiness giver
Roblox player
Runner adorer
Sprout hater
Wonky teeth hater.

Layla Adams (8)
Tickton CE Primary School, Tickton

This Is Me
A kennings poem

Chocolate orange muncher
Cat squirter
Doughnut crusher
Nice biker
Funny joker
Coconut cruncher
Spider squisher
Toffee squealer
Happy hugger
Snake hater
Silly bouncer
Pink lover
Scar hider.

Lily Coates (7)
Tickton CE Primary School, Tickton

This Is Me
A kennings poem

School hater
Hero petter
Spider lover
Mosquito flicker
Ice cream licker
Weekend lay-in-er
Heat sweater
Finger biter
Clumsy walker
Broccoli spitter
Strong lifter
Main dancer
Lazy chiller.

Bobby Butler (7)
Tickton CE Primary School, Tickton

This Is Me
A kennings poem

Games player
Running lover
Sweets muncher
Good glitcher
Scar builder
Funny laughter
Dirt hider
Mud hater
Diving stopper
Nice creator
Technology gamer
Walking stepper
Entertaining runner.

Henry Fisher (7)
Tickton CE Primary School, Tickton

All About Me
A kennings poem

Thorn dodger
Web hater
Cut ranter
Slug poker
Happy grinner
Mathematic lover
Energetic runner
Fast sprinter
Hair fiddler
Magic liker
Sour sweet chewer
Pokémon watcher
Snow thrower.

Arthur Hornby (7)
Tickton CE Primary School, Tickton

This Is Me!
A kennings poem

Beach splasher
Travelling hater
Dog lover
Fight disliker
Cat fighter
Youngest hater
Sunshine layer
Football player
Energetic runner
Art drawer
Hair hitter
Smile lover
Friendly smiler.

Tom Jebson (7)
Tickton CE Primary School, Tickton

This Is Me!
A kennings poem

Art lover
Bookshelf tidier
Clumsiness worrier
Enthusiastic helper
Fly flicker
Lego builder
Rain hater
Scrambled egg scoffer
Silly joker
Sprout despiser
Video game player
Weekend lazer.

Logan Butler (8)
Tickton CE Primary School, Tickton

This Is Me!
A kennings poem

Dog walker
Football player
Friend smiler
Beach swimmer
Spider screamer
Bed lazer
Seagull scarer
Rain hider
Funny joker
Energetic runner
Kind hugger
Happy friend
Exercise sweater.

Daisy Cowell (7)
Tickton CE Primary School, Tickton

This Is Me
A kennings poem

Friendly player
Chocolate drooler
Sick crier
Silly joker
Sweaty runner
Snot lover
Warts annoyer
Cheeky grinner
Slime poker
Funny smiler
Snake scarer
Winter thrower
Spider hater.

Phoebe Gibson (7)
Tickton CE Primary School, Tickton

This Is Me!
A kennings poem

Friend carer
Playful learner
Chatterbox chatterer
Chicken lover
Swimming player
Friend lover
Duvet taker
Candyfloss eater
Dark morning avoider
Bogies hater
Tired layer
Silly worrier.

Mollie Gillyon (8)
Tickton CE Primary School, Tickton

This Is Me!
A kennings poem

Cat stroker
Dog hugger
Hamster player
Water lover
Coffee spitter
Spider screamer
Wasp scarer
Bugs hater
Kind smiler
Respectful lover
Helpful helper
Caring hugger
Tired sleeper.

Miley Wright (7)
Tickton CE Primary School, Tickton

This Is Me!
A kennings poem

Karate liker
EJ smiler
Happy talker
Old hater
Bad manners upsetter
Good friend hugger
Rain hater
Silly joker
Heights crier
Coffee spitter
Kind smiler
Friends player
Mum lover.

Frankie Sheppard (7)
Tickton CE Primary School, Tickton

My Poem
A kennings poem

Happy smiler
Shy singer
Dog owner
Snow freezer
Watermelon sicker
Sister lover
Tomato spitter
Cucumber hater
Biscuit nibbler
Friend hugger
Kind talker
School lover
Cat sleeper.

Ava Melling (7)
Tickton CE Primary School, Tickton

This Is Me!
A kennings poem

Chocolate stuffer
Coffee lover
Lazy sleeper
Bin hider
Spider liker
Heights screamer
Cool biker
Silly sleeper
Wind despiser
Coldness hater
Wart hater
Weekend eater
Xbox hogger.

Myles Musgrave (7)
Tickton CE Primary School, Tickton

This Is Me
A kennings poem

Cat petter
Happy helper
Chocolate spitter
Wart wearer
Lovely hugger
Friendly smiler
Funny lover
Dog hater
Rain disguiser
Sunshine hider
Beach layer
iPad lover
Candy stealer.

Emmy Harrison Saunders (7)
Tickton CE Primary School, Tickton

This Is Me!
A kennings poem

Dog walker
Glue sticker
Kind sharer
Hand rubber
Chocolate eater
Coffee spitter
Lift freezer
Lazy sleeper
Beach splasher
Happy player
Sunshine layer
Neck holder
Spider hater.

Poppy Smith (7)
Tickton CE Primary School, Tickton

This Is Me
A kennings poem

Being poorly disliker
Dog adorer
Fast swimmer
Gap teeth hater
Happy liver
Hot chocolate drinker
Music listener
Puppy lover
Rat escaper
Spider avoider
Snake hater
Wasp detester.

Anna Gibson (8)
Tickton CE Primary School, Tickton

This Is Me!
A kennings poem

Wasp detester
Tennis player
Tall disliker
Swimming liker
Spider escaper
Music listener
Harry Potter reader
Glasses wearer
Friend protector
Dog lover
Dark disliker
Calm learner.

Alissia Williams (9)
Tickton CE Primary School, Tickton

This Is Me!
A kennings poem

Chickenpox hater
Friend maker
Hamster lover
Lazy sleeper
Long hair wanter
Mean people detester
Mess maker
Rat escaper
Roblox gamer
Sleepover taker
Sweet sneaker
Snake avoider.

Rosie Smith (9)
Tickton CE Primary School, Tickton

This Is Me!
A kennings poem

Football player
Dog lover
Birthday liker
Fortnite gamer
Snot avoider
Snake escaper
Cheese hater
Wasp detester
Bee attacker
Fly flicker
Classroom tidier
Having glasses hater.

Riley Coates (8)
Tickton CE Primary School, Tickton

This Is Me
A kennings poem

Kind helper
Silly joker
Happy hugger
Funny laugher
Wind runner
Friend liker
Family lover
Sun layer
Spider squatter
Slug squasher
Billy hater
Beer spitter
Scab picker.

Henry Leek (7)
Tickton CE Primary School, Tickton

This Is Me
A kennings poem

Bunny petter
Scar hider
Silly joker
Rose liker
Sun hater
Wine spitter
Energetic jumper
Kind helper
Clover looker
Shark runner
Cold lover
Lazy layer
Life seeker.

Phoebe Dawson (7)
Tickton CE Primary School, Tickton

This Is Me!
A kennings poem

Dog petter
Glue sticker
Tea lover
Water splasher
Smart thinker
Tall hater
Lazy layer
Beach player
Smiley singer
Happy hugger
Life hider
Roller coaster screamer.

Chantelle Stewart (8)
Tickton CE Primary School, Tickton

This Is Me

A kennings poem

Football player
Fortnite gamer
Hot dog muncher
Mess maker
Running racer
Joke teller
Dark escaper
Orange juice avoider
Bumpy skin disliker
Being left out detester.

Ted Plant (9)
Tickton CE Primary School, Tickton

This Is Me!
A kennings poem

Dog lover
Joke teller
Blister hater
Roblox player
Pasta eater
Snot avoider
Harry Potter reader
Animal carer
Friend protector
Birthday liker
Bee lover.

Ella Hadley (8)
Tickton CE Primary School, Tickton

This Is Me

A kennings poem

Happy hugger
Wind hater
Beach layer
Lazy layer
Dad teaser
Sun lover
Fling mover
Bear hater
Coach hater
Sport runner
Cheese monster
Mum hugger.

Annie Moody (7)
Tickton CE Primary School, Tickton

This Is Me!
A kennings poem

PlayStation gamer
Funny joker
Patient waiter
Lazy runner
Climbing lover
Swimming hater
Heights scared
Itch scratcher
Cliffs looker
Sport golfer.

Jack Cawkwell-Jeffrey (7)
Tickton CE Primary School, Tickton

This Is Me!
A kennings poem

Dog lover
Ice cream licker
Bee hater
Swimming liker
Fast runner
Playground smiler
Shoe hater
Family lover
Cheek giver
Wasp detester.

Lyla Thomson (8)
Tickton CE Primary School, Tickton

This Is Me!
A kennings poem

Dog lover
Family hugger
Roblox gamer
Football scorer
Picture sketcher
Gardening digger
Bogey avoider
Tuna disliker
Tomato hater.

Hollie Taggart (8)
Tickton CE Primary School, Tickton

This Is Me

A kennings poem

Video player
Lasagne avoider
Pig master
Fun maker
Country catcher
Fortnite player
English escaper
Allergy hater
Animal adorer.

Sebby Holmes Rodmell (8)
Tickton CE Primary School, Tickton

This Is Me!
A kennings poem

Music listener
Christmas lover
Puppy adorer
Bee disliker
Bed overtaker
Crowd hater
Hair colour disliker.

Isla Murphy (8)
Tickton CE Primary School, Tickton

This Is Me!
A kennings poem

Bike rider
Sports player
Clock ticker
Shark avoider
Trampoline bouncer
Tuna, sprout and carrot hater.

Charlie Hague (8)
Tickton CE Primary School, Tickton

It's Cupcake O'Clock

As I look out of my window I see the sun shining as bright as a star,
I head into the kitchen as it's cupcake o'clock!
I gather all of my ingredients together and begin,
First we add a sprinkle of love,
A drizzle of smiles,
A cupful of happiness
And mix it all together,
I then evenly dish out into pretty cases to pop in the oven,
The sweet aroma fills the kitchen
And makes me feel warm and happy as I pass the oven,
The glass reminds me of a new shining penny,
I open with care and then decorate with finishing touches,
Now it's cupcake o'clock!

Layla Williams (9)
Ysgol Cae Top, Bangor

Me

I am a girl in this world
I am a music player
In my mind I have a dream to be an astronaut
To explore unknown planets in other solar systems
I have two younger brothers and I was born before them
I don't have any older brothers or sisters
I was born first
One of my brothers is two years old and the other one is six
I love them a lot, more than anything else in this world
I am nine years old and I love music and I am called Sofia.

Sofia Roque-Nunes (9)
Ysgol Cae Top, Bangor

This Is Me

I am very small
I am not a stranger to football
And like to fall
From the climbing wall.

I am very strong
And full of song
And like to run along the big pontoon
Plus I never get things wrong.

I am very sporty
And a bit of a shorty
And sometimes go pianoforte
Just like I ought to.

My favourite colour is pink
And I like leopard print
There's no time to think
'Cause there's washing in the sink.

It won't go away
And I want to play
In the park today
So I am on my way.

Evangeline Goodwin (10)
Ysgol Cae Top, Bangor

I Am A Fox

I am a fox,
As red as can be,
A riddle to the eye,
As I am a shape-shifter,
My emerald eyes gleam in the dark.

I am a fox,
As stealthy as can be,
A darting shadow in the twilight gloom,
There is no point in trying to catch me,
My silver spirit is free.

I am a girl,
With fox in me,
I dash down my street at lightning speed,
I startle at this human clatter.

Hazel Story (10)
Ysgol Cae Top, Bangor

Football, Football, Football

Dribbling, dashing, defending
Sprinting, striding, saving
Passing, playing, possessing.

Balls, boots, bottles
Stadium, studs, substitutes
Goals, goalkeepers, goalposts.

Rooney, Ramsey, Ronaldo
Mbappé, Moore, Messi
Salah, Suarez, Sanchez.

Football, football, football.

Osian Layton (9)
Ysgol Cae Top, Bangor

That's Me!

F un and friendly
L aughing all day
O nly one of her kind
R ing her up and tell her
A nything on your mind.

C alm and cool
A wesomely helpful
R eading all the time
R eally likes animals
E ndings can rhyme!

Flora Carré (9)
Ysgol Cae Top, Bangor

About Me And My Family

My family is small but that means all
My dad is tall
My mum is short
My sisters are little but they mean all
My dad goes to work and he comes home when it is dark
When we are free we play in parks
We have a dog
All day it barks
My family is small but that means all.

Abirami Nadarajah (9)
Ysgol Cae Top, Bangor

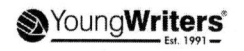

YOUNG WRITERS INFORMATION

We hope you have enjoyed reading this book – and that you will continue to in the coming years.

If you're the parent or family member of an enthusiastic poet or story writer, do visit our website **www.youngwriters.co.uk/subscribe** and sign up to receive news, competitions, writing challenges and tips, activities and much, much more! There's lots to keep budding writers motivated!

If you would like to order further copies of this book, or any of our other titles, then please give us a call or order via your online account.

Young Writers
Remus House
Coltsfoot Drive
Peterborough
PE2 9BF
(01733) 890066
info@youngwriters.co.uk

Join in the conversation!
Tips, news, giveaways and much more!

YoungWritersUK   **YoungWritersCW**   **youngwriterscw**